CW00449353

1

For Aurelia, my inspiration for change and encouraging understanding and compassion for the world and the entirety of its inhabitants.

Vera & Bob

Elizabeth P Burakevic

Contents

Introduction

Vera is Six years old and she lives with her Mummy, a behavioural scientist, and the Daddy, an architect from Russia, on a little farm in the New Forest, England. Vera was a very clever little girl that spoke English and Russian **fluently** but she was quite shy; she was cautious with new people and often hid behind her mum when strangers stopped to stare at her beautiful big eyes. However, she was very at home in nature and loved playing on the farm and running barefoot around the garden then laying on the cool grass while **Krolik** (Russian word for rabbit) groomed her face with his little tongue and climbing the tree fort she built with her Daddy when they first moved to the farm. She did not think life could get anymore perfect, that is until the day of her Seventh birthday…

Vera

1 – Bob

It was a cool, grey morning, water trickled out of the tap on the old trough, Vera woke excited, threw her jumper and boots over her pyjamas and scurried over to the feed barn where Mummy was soaking the sugar out of the hay and mixing the medicines and **supplements** into the feed for the older or sick horses and poor doers (the term used to describe horses that loose a lot of weight in the winter or have trouble gaining it back)

'Good morning birthday girl!' said mummy, 'jump on the trailer, you can feed the horses with me, then I have a surprise for you'.

Vera often helped her mummy feed and check the horses in the morning, but today was different; they stopped at a small side paddock that they normally used for **quarantine**, when a new animal arrived, to make sure it was not sick and going to infect the other animals.

'Move quietly and slowly and go look through the fence' said Vera's mummy.

There in the corner, was a scruffy little pony, no more than Nine hands high (measurement specific to horses and equal to 10.16cm or 4inches), big thick mane that almost covered his eyes and thin with a big scar that reached from his ribs, across his shoulder and on to the top of his left leg.

'What is wrong with him?' Vera asked her mother

Bob

'He is frightened' said Mummy

'No, I mean what happened to his side?' said Vera

'He was found by a member of the public, tangled in barb wire, in the Forest, it took 150 stitches to repair the wound but the damage is on the inside now, in his mind. He will be a good little pony for you, if you are willing to learn and nurse him' explained Mummy
'Really?!' said Vera excitedly

'Yes, but you have to spend time with him every day and it is going to take intelligent forward planning and **patience**' said Mummy

'I can do it, I can do it, I promise' beamed Vera as she jumped up and down **enthusiastically**

'I know you can, we will start tomorrow' said Mummy smiling.

> **word of the day:**
> Patience - (noun): quiet, steady perseverance; even-tempered care; to work with patience.
> Enthusiastic - (adjective): from the noun enthusiasm; absorbing or controlling possession of the mind by any interest or pursuit; lively interest.

2 – Habituation

That morning Vera was so excited that she knocked the clock on the floor as she tried to stop the alarm, hurried down the stairs, put on her boots and ran across to the feed barn.

'Good morning mummy' she panted, 'so what are we doing... brushing, riding, lunging?'

Vera's Mummy smiled quietly.

'This morning you are going to sit in the field and read this book' she said

Traditional Lunging

'is that it?!' exclaimed Vera 'how is that horse training?'

'Bob is very frightened and needs time to get used to you so that he can see you don't intend to eat or hurt him' Mummy explained

'Eww! I'm not going to eat him, why would he think that?!' Vera said in horror

'Horses are prey animals and humans are **predators**, he can tell by the way your eyes are facing forward, to help you judge the distance and size of things in front of you, compared to prey animals whose eyes are normally on the side of their heads, to give them a broader field of vision. This means horses can see almost all the way around them but they can not be sure if something is really big but far away, or really small but close' said Mummy

Mummy continued to explain that this was the reason why horses sometimes jump when they see an object like a plastic bag, moving on the road; if they did not start running straight away, and it did turn out to be a **predator**, the **predator** would gain the advantage and potentially catch them.

'Ohhh, that makes sense, but so many people say they are stupid for doing that' said Vera

'Yes, but they are actually very clever, it is just that people do not understand. After all it is better to be wrong than be eaten' said mummy.

So Vera sat reading her book and she sat there the next day and the day after that until Bob didn't pay any attention to her presence and just acted normally; pottering about eating hay and grass. On day five mummy decided he was relaxed enough for them to take in the wheel barrow and clean up all the poop that had been mounting up since he had arrived. They also put a box of brushes on the floor and hung the head collar and rope on the gate to allow Bob to explore these new items at his own pace and in an environment to which he was acclimatised.

[At this point it is worth explaining that Vera is home educated. Mummy would take any topic that Vera was interested in (normally animals) and use it to teach all subjects like science, history, math, English, art and more; that way Vera absorbed much more information because she did not find it boring. Learning to train Bob would teach Vera animal behaviour, **anatomy**, art (from drawing him) language and creativity (from reading to him) and the art of patience, amongst other skills such as husbandry, planning and environmental sciences.]

Every morning for the next week Vera cleaned up the poop and gave Bob fresh food and water and every afternoon she sat in the corner with a book or her pad and pencils and practised drawing Bob paying special attention to his facial expressions. Mummy had set up a video camera to record Bob's progress so Vera would speak out loud for the camera to record her observations. One day Vera was crouched down picking up the brushes that bob had knocked all over the floor and Bob came up behind her; lightly touching her back, she reached her hand around slowly until she was touching his nose, then slowly turned around to look at him, she remembered mummy saying that staring at him in the eyes is aggressive and frightening, so she just looked down past his nose to his shoulder, she gently stroked his face, always keeping contact and touching him with flat hands so they did not resemble claws, then she walked away, climbed over the field gate and ran as fast as she could to the house to tell mummy and daddy.

'That is excellent' said Daddy

'Well done for not pushing him too fast and for ending on a positive note' said mummy proudly.

---

word of the day:
Anatomy - (noun) the structure of an animal or plant, or part of it.

---

3 – Learning Theory

word of the day:
Incentive - (noun): something that incites action or greater effort, as a reward offered for increased productivity.

By the end of the next week Bob was enjoying being brushed all over his fluffy body. As it was a nice clear day and Bob seemed relaxed Vera decided to try to put on the head collar; she wanted to get him used to being led and tied up and so she could safely get him used to having his hooves picked up and cleaned; he was going to need the farrier soon as they were getting long where the soft spongy grass was not wearing them down like the hard and stony tracks did when he freely roamed the New Forest.

'Hello Bob' she said quietly 'would you like to put this on please'

She presented the head collar and tried to get it on his nose, Bob took one look, lifted his head high, put his ears back and reversed before spinning and trotting away. Vera tried again and again but no luck.

'Uh… he won't do it!' she complained to her mother who was stood watching at the gate.

'He will; he just needs the right **incentive**. Let's take a break and I can explain a bit about learning theory and reinforcement while we eat lunch' said mummy.

Vera and her mummy went back to the kitchen where there was a lovely pasta and lentil bake waiting.

'Now, Learning Theory might seem a little boring but it is important for you to know so you can identify and understand behaviour and training. All animals, including humans learn the same, it is just that the results can differ slightly because of species and individual past experience, as well as personality' Mummy explained as she reached for Vera's notepad and pen. 'Conditioning is what we call it when an animal learns to respond a certain way, after being regularly exposed to a specific **stimulus** or situation; this happens naturally and is how we work out stuff like which food is safe and yummy and which food will make us sick... The most likely reason Bob ran away from the head collar is that something bad happened when he was caught before, it might even be because he was free roaming and then he was caught, injected with **sedative** and had his painful wound stitched up...'

'But that was to help him and save his life!' said Vera interrupting

'... he doesn't know that, he just remembers it being scary' said Mummy 'being frightened of the head collar because of a bad memory is caused by Second Order Conditioning, another example is how the horses all come to the fence when I go to the feed barn, they know that food is on the way. This chain of events can grow and grow when the horse notices a pattern and can become a problem as they might react badly to something we consider silly or even dangerous as they remember that thing normally leads to something they don't like.'

Mummy drew four boxes with two R's in and two P's in and explained that;

'Positive Punishment (+P) is not nice punishment like it sounds, it means you add something unpleasant after the horse does something you don't want, in the belief that the horse will connect the two events and remember not to do it anymore'

'That does not sound very nice!' said Vera

---

word of the day:
Stimulus - (noun): something that incites to action or exertion or quickens action, feeling, thought, etc.
Sedative - (noun) drug/medicine given to keep patient still.

Quadrants of Reinforcement

'It isn't and it also takes quite lot of repeated punishment for the horse to understand which can damage the relationship and trust between horse and human, but it used to be the normal way of training and is still unfortunately how some trainers and riders aim to get results' said Mummy 'Think of how many times you heard people say "get on and give him a good kick and smack with the whip, he is being disrespectful", when really the horse might be in pain or trying to tell you something is wrong. You might not remember because you were so small but people said this to me a lot about Spartacus, but I did not listen, I retired him because I knew he was an honest horse, and now look at him, stiff as a board if he doesn't have his pain medication and physiotherapy. Horses speak a lot, but you have to be ready to listen and work together; it is a privilege they let us ride them not our right!' proclaimed Mummy with tears in her eyes 'and it is one reason many horses develop problems and get sold or abandoned; because they become dangerous'.

'So is −P when you take the punishment away?' asked Vera

'Good effort, but no, it is actually when you take something nice away after an unwanted behaviour, like when some parents take away their child's toys for doing something naughty; that wouldn't work with a horse so you take away a resource that the horse needs, like water, food or the ability to play or interact with others, which is very dangerous for their health as they could get stomach ulcers from not eating regularly and also stress like this can lead to stereotypies' (also known as stable vices, are an un-natural behaviour the horse starts doing because it can't do what it wants/needs or is bored or stressed). Explained Mummy

Mummy continued to say how Negative Reinforcement (-R) is a big part of what many people call 'Natural Horsemanship' and is arguably the movement that helped many people start to re-think how horses were trained.

'It is when you apply unpleasant pressure or an aversive stimulus until the horse does what you want and then you immediately release or remove that aversive, for example: if you pull the lead rope to ask your horse to walk forward and stop pulling when he starts moving, or if you put your hand on his side and start to push him, asking for him to move over. Applying pressure, if used wisely is fine, but it is not without its problems and some very sensitive horses can become more frightened and dangerous or depressed. An event is recalled differently by everyone involved; think about when you are riding, you squeeze or kick your legs and the horse starts walking, you experience Positive Reinforcement because he did what you asked, but your horse experienced negative reinforcement because you stopped kicking when he walked forward' she said.

'So what can you do?' asked Vera

'Well, it is best to try and start with Positive Reinforcement (+R), then both you and the horse have happy experiences being together, improving your bond and it makes the horse smarter as you encourage them to think and solve problems by offering you different behaviours in hope of a reward' said Mummy.

Mummy explained how +R (also known as clicker training or bridge training) is very popular in dog training and training wild animals both in zoos, to be able to give them health checks or medicine without stress, and by many modern animal trainers who train animals to perform in films. The click is used to mark the exact behaviour the animal did that you wanted because it is difficult to deliver the reward quickly enough that the animal doesn't confuse the reward for something else. She also pointed out the risk of training too many things and over controlling the horses behaviour, like training a horse that has been greeting you with a grumpy face and ears pinned back, to put their ears forward…

'Training little communication behaviours like this can make it difficult to read how the horse is truly feeling… like wearing a mask, so as with all methods of training it should be used carefully with an emphasis on freedom of choice and mutual cooperation and benefit' said Mummy 'training prey animals like horses is very different to training predators like dogs because dogs naturally have to think of ways to catch their food, whereas grass and plants do not try and run way from the horse.'

Vera laughed.

'…and if you don't tend to spend lots of time just being outside with your horse, it can be helpful to wear something visual like a specific item of clothing or a treat bag so they know when rewards are available; this will help prevent them offering behaviours like the Spanish Walk or turning his hips towards you when it might not be safe or you aren't prepared; safety is very important which is why you must always wear proper shoes and your helmet when you are near the horses. When you start clicker training it is best to start from behind a fence or stable door/ door chain, this way you are safe from the horse crowding you and trying to bully the food out of you before they learn the rules, but also, if the horse is nervous…' said mummy.

'Like Bob' Vera added

'Yes like Bob, he will feel safe because he can see you won't be able to hurt him, some horses who have been trained using punishment or aversives can be very frightened of getting told off for giving the wrong answer' explained Mummy.

Vera and her Mummy wrote down the goals they wanted to achieve with Bob and then they wrote step by step instructions, with small steps in between goals, of how to shape his behaviour and introduce him gradually to each task.

'You have to set him up to succeed… there is no point expecting him to understand and achieve a big goal straight away as he will get worried and run away or stop trying and we must keep the sessions short, ending on a good point, then for the first few weeks we repeat the lesson a lot, gradually increasing the gap between that lesson and introducing new tasks, so that it gets ingrained in his memory, once we are sure he has learnt it, it just needs repeating every so often to stop it getting extinguished over time' said Mummy.

Mummy then drew another diagram of five boxes on the pad containing letters 'C', 'FI', 'FR', 'VI', 'VR' whilst Vera finished her pasta bake and tried pouring herself some elderflower water without spilling it all over the table.

Just then there was a loud knock on the door, it was Vera's music teacher arriving for her lesson. "come in, we won't be a minute" said mummy opening the door.

Spanish Walk

'The last thing to quickly look at, for now, is the Rate of Reinforcement; this is the rate at which you give the horse a reward. 'C' stands for continuous and is how most +R trainers start with. Just using CR is thought to increase the likelihood of the behaviour being extinguished and forgotten and it makes it harder to remove the constant need to reward once the behaviour is established; think about how you would feel if every time Grandma came she gave you pocket money or sweets and then one day she just stopped; you would feel disappointed because you had gotten used to receiving them every time she came. Fixed Interval (FI) is when the reward is delivered at a set time, like every two minutes, Fixed Ratio is after a set amount of correct behaviours, like the horse giving the correct answer three times, both of these are too predictable as the horse will recognise the pattern and slow down his effort after the last reward as he knows he wont be getting a reward the next time. Variable Ratio is the best as the horse will keep trying as he won't know if the reward is coming on the next attempt or in two attempts. Alternatively if it is a difficult task we can give a reward each time or give him a special reward, known as a jackpot' said mummy.

'Wow I'm exhausted!' said Vera

'It was a lot of information' laughed Mummy 'have a break and go to your piano practise and then we will give it a try'

'YES' said Vera excitedly.

> **word of the day:**
> Jackpot - (noun): training term to describe a large or high level reward, given to mark extra special behaviour or the end of a training session (when given at the end of a session it is usually put on the floor as it lowers the head and encourages the horse to go back to grazing while you walk away).

4 – Practise

That afternoon the sun was bright and warm and all the animals were dozing, Vera and her Mummy marched out to Bob's paddock armed with treat bags, helmets, back protectors and yard boots. Inside the treat bag was an array of sweet feed, linseed cakes, carrot sticks and pony nuts. Mummy took the head collar and started to demonstrate, while Vera stood to the side. At first Mummy walked toward Bob and when she was about two metres away she stopped and turned sideways to him while she explained what she was doing.

'Turning my back or my shoulder to him and looking away lets him know I don't want to attack him… a horse with his tail towards you is defensive but still dangerous if you don't listen to what his body language is saying, this is why I like turning my shoulder to him as, in his mind, I am not likely to kick him that way' said Mummy.

Whilst Mummy had been talking Bob had come up behind her to investigate.

'He is curious' said Vera.

Mummy turned to show the head collar, holding it just in front of him until he turned his head forward and had his ears facing the head collar, then she made a click noise and lowered the head collar and gave him a piece of carrot, she did this a few times until he stopped looking away, then she brought it closer and onto his nose, then took it off again straight away and repeated this, each time increasing the length of time she held it on his nose and clicking every time he stayed calm. Eventually she fastened the head collar behind his ears, clicked and gave him a big handful of carrots and sweet feed as a marker for very good behaviour, and then she took it off again.

'Right, your turn Vera' she said handing Vera the head collar.

Vera walked towards Bob taking big slow breaths, she remembers the book she had read about controlling your breathing to help slow your heart beat and stay calm because horses had super sensitive hearing and could hear your heart beat (and tell you are scared) from metres away; because they live in herds they get frightened if another horse (herd member) is scared, as it might mean danger. Vera did exactly as her mother had done and it was a complete success; Bob wasn't at all phased.

'I did it!' she said beaming a big smile from ear to ear and trying to contain her happiness.

'Well done' said her mother 'we will finish for today, the other animals need feeding and you need to get ready for bed, while you sleep your brain will start to make sense of and store all the new information you have learnt today.'

For the next week Vera continued to work with Bob, every morning and evening teaching him to stand still, picking up his feet and improving his handling and manners, always making sure he had his head facing forward and her hand away from her body with fingers flat and together when giving his food reward to make sure he remembered to respect the **personal space** boundary that she had set and not nip at her or get rough. In the afternoon she still sat reading, drawing his body postures and facial expressions or making plans for the next training sessions. Vera decided it was time to start lunging Bob and training him to move his body when she asked but she needed Mummy's help.

'Mummy, how do I ask him to walk backwards and sideways without forcing him?' she asked.
'If we were to use Negative Reinforcement, we would apply pressure with our hand, to his chest and maybe his lead rope and as soon as he moved back we would stop pushing' explained Mummy

'But I want to use Positive Reinforcement' said Vera

'OK, the easiest way with +R is to use target training and we ask the opposite of moving away... come on, I will show you' said Mummy picking up an old fly swatter and walking out to the field.

'Just like we did with the head collar, you hold the target quietly in front of the body part you want him to touch it with, we will start with his nose as it is easy, remember not to move it suddenly because of the horses eyesight they might think you are going to hit them with it. When he touches the target, you click and reward. When he has mastered one body part you can move on to the next, like his leg, if you hold it close enough, eventually he should move and touch it accidentally, then you can reward and repeat, he will soon get the hang of it' said Mummy.

Target touching

'So if I want him to back up' said Vera taking the fly swatter from her Mum, 'I put the target under his nose and move it towards his chest?' she asked

As she moved the target Bob started to back up, trying to touch the target with his nose.

'Click and reward Vera' said Mummy urgently.

'He did it' said Vera

Mummy smiled and nodded 'Another way to train him that works well when you spend as much time as you do is called Capturing, you just wait until he does something you want him to do, like going to the toilet, click, reward, every time he goes to the toilet when you are there you repeat until you have captured the behaviour'.

Mummy explained that getting him to go to the toilet on command can be useful if you ever need to get a sample for the vet, or worm egg counts. The next day Vera continued as she had been, training in the morning and evening in a few short sessions, broken up by feeding, grooming and mucking out the field and in the afternoons; studying and sketching his behaviour or planning how to use her new skills. On the following Monday, Mummy came walking up the lane with William (the conqueror, to use his full name, although not a name he lived up to.) he was a middle ranking gelding from the good doer bachelor herd, there were four herds on the farm, all rescued apart from Sparticus. They were divided into mixed (mares and geldings), bachelor (just geldings) and then poor or good doers (how well they maintain weight), splitting them like this mimicked how they grouped themselves in the wild and meant it was easier for Mummy to manage feeding times and grazing.

> **terms of the day:**
> **Worm-egg count** - a test that identifies type and quantity of parasites in a given poop sample.
> **Gelding** - a neutered male horse.

'What are you doing with William Mummy?' Vera asked.

'It will soon be time for Bob to join the herd so he needs to make a friend before hand, to stop him getting bullied by the bossy ones' said Mummy 'horses tend to make a pair bond with other horses that are similar to them, so William should be perfect and together they will rank higher in the herd because they will watch out for each other and share resources... We are having some big improvements made to the fields so it will be perfect timing to introduce them back into the herd once the work is finished at the end of next week'.

William had a quick sniff of Bob through the gate and seeing as neither seemed bothered by each other, Mummy let him loose and they were left to get used to each other for the rest of the day.

5 – Track systems

The next morning Vera went out to see Bob and William, they were grazing peacefully next to each other.

'Bob' she called,

But Bob did not come, she could see he heard her because his ear turned to face her, but he did not come over like normal. Just then Mummy came walking out of the house with a tall blonde lady that Vera recognised from the local dog charity that Mummy had volunteered at.

'Hello Vera, you remember my friend Elsa? She used to be an Animal Rights lawyer back in Sweden and she founded the New Forest Hope dog charity I helped at a few months ago' said Mummy introducing the lady.

'Hello' said Vera quietly 'Mummy, Bob isn't coming to me when I call him' she said disappointed.

'He is just getting used to William, keep sitting with them, doing your drawings and he will come to you when he has established his bond with his new friend. In fact, you could use the time to draw the different interactions between Bob and William, to learn how the horses talk to each other' replied Mummy, but for now, why don't you come with us and see what we are doing to the rest of the farm?'

'Ok' said Vera.

As they walked down the stony lane Elsa said to Vera:

'I think it is great, what you are doing with Bob… I use Positive Reinforcement with the dogs at the shelter, when they have been through such bad experiences with people it is a great way to help them trust again'.

'Thank you' said Vera 'I am hoping to be able to ride him soon, he let me put a little saddle on him and Mummy has started helping me longrein'

'That is great, are you in any pony clubs or groups?' asked Elsa

'No, when I have started talking to other people about how I train Bob and that our horses don't wear shoes or live in stables, most people just laugh or tell me I'm stupid' said Vera dismayed.

'There will always be critics, and it is normal for people to laugh or dismiss things that they don't understand, but that is exactly why I think you should go to competitions or do some demonstrations and show what you can do, the more people see what can be achieved the more they might have a go, you just have to think of a way to tell people without them thinking you are saying they are not caring for their horses properly… like explaining how good it is for fighting boredom if their horse has to stay in a stable for a long time due to injury' encouraged Elsa.

'Do you think so? I think I'm a way off that yet' said Vera in a shy voice.

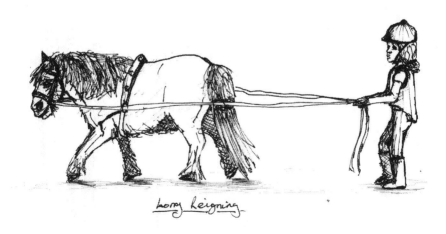

Pony Reigning

'Maybe next year you will be more confident, I can look in to some events after Christmas if you like?' said Mummy

Just then they reached the entrance to the horse fields, there were people dragging posts and trees around and diggers making mud mounds and shallow ditches.

'Wow, what are they doing?' Vera asked

'They are building a track with lots of natural stimulus to encourage the horses to move and forage, **mimicking** more natural habitat and behaviours' said Mummy pulling out a big map of the field. 'Each track and paddock is having silver birch trees planted for natural shade and for health benefits if they want to eat it, a sand pit for rolling and a comfortable place to lay, various spots with hay at different heights, a herb garden, water trough and stream or pool to drink and bathe in, hard standing in the large open door barn to keep dry if they want to, a stony area and logs laid out to help them harden their feet and encourage them to lift their legs and exercise over the logs.'

'It is a massive project. What are you doing about the big oak trees that are poisonous to the horses?' asked Elsa

'The tree trunk will be fenced off to stop them eating the bark and when the acorns start to drop in the autumn the pigs will be let out on the track to eat them up, fortunately we don't have any syca-more or other large toxic trees but we will be using the sheep and alpacas to manage the weeds' explained Mummy

'But where is all the grass?! I thought horses needed lots of grass to eat?' exclaimed Vera

> **word of the day:**
> Mimicking - (noun): a copy or imitation of something.

'The Poor Doers will get time in the pockets of pasture fenced off in their paddocks but horses come from countries with poor grass that is dry and bristly, it is better for them to have lots of good hay and browse on the other plants in the field' said Mummy

'Yes, spring and autumn grass can be quite dangerous for horses because it has a lot of sugar in it that can damage their feet and make them fat' added Elsa

'Oh! But won't the gravel and stones hurt their feet?' Vera asked

'Not too much,' said Mummy 'because none of our horses wear metal shoes, giving them hard and varied surfaces to walk on, instead of just soft grass, helps them to get used to the feeling… they can go slowly until they are used to the conditions and before they have to carry the weight of a rider'

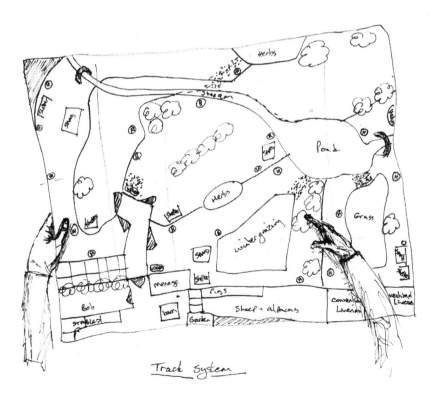

Track System

'Wouldn't it just be easier to put metal shoes on?' asked Vera

'Perhaps, but the metal shoes affect the natural design of the hoof, stopping the digital cushion contacting the floor and the spread of the hoof at the back. The horses hoof is designed to absorb concussion and protect the joints in the rest of the body; a bit like trying to jump up and down without bending your knees or like the difference between jumping on a trampoline or on the pavement; it can hurt, but more importantly, over time it damages the joints and can make more problems in the future' said Mummy

The other horses had been put in the holding paddocks for a few days whilst the fencing was completed and for collecting poop samples before worming. Inspired by Elsa's talk of using positive reinforcement to prevent boredom in confined horses, Vera thought it the perfect opportunity to introduce them to target training, using the protective contact of the wooden fence. Some picked it up very quickly, mainly the lower ranking and younger ones who had seen her teaching the higher ranking ones next to them. A couple of the older ones had been through tough times and were reluctant to try something new in case they got told off. Vera just took it slow and

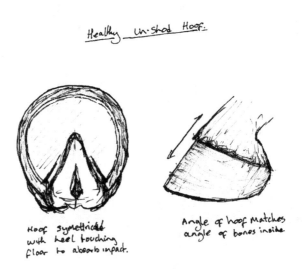

Healthy Un-shod Hoof.

Hoof symethrical with heel touching floor to absorb impact.

Angle of hoof matches angle of bones inside.

Avoidance

asked for little, easy behaviours. Bob had come around too and was back to his regular learning pace, he even let Vera sit on him and be calmly led around.

The day came when the track system was complete and it was time to put all the horses back out, including Bob and William, which was going to make Vera's training a little more challenging, she would have to catch and bring him out of the field so the other horses couldn't come and try to steal the food from her treat bag. Mummy had been up early, worming the ones that needed it and she had called in back up and extra help in case something went wrong; Daddy was there and Grandma the nurse (in case some-body got hurt), Elsa and her husband Theo, who happened to be the farms Vet, and Babushka (Grandma in Russian) who was a photographer and had come to document the event and try to get some beautiful and animated shots of the horses exploring their new homes. Herd by herd they were released and all took off for a good gallop, bucking and jumping around playfully before stopping to sniff and investigate. Then came the turn of the Good Doer

Bachelors, all together the horses were led into the enclosure and lead ropes removed (the head collars were left on in case Bob needed catching and removing to safety), they took off running, all except Bob who was not quite sure, the other horses came back and started sniffing at him, William stood by him for support and after a few squeals and foreleg strike threats, they all ran off together, rolling in the sand pit and splashing in the stream. It was a success.

word of the day:
Concussion - (noun): shock caused by the impact of a collision, blow, etc
Protective Contact - interacting with free roaming animals behind the safety of a barrier.
Gallop - (noun) a fast gait of the horse or other quadruped in which, in the course of each stride, all four feet are off the ground at once.
Bucking - (verb): (of a saddle or pack animal) to leap with arched back and come down with head low and forelegs stiff, in order to dislodge a rider or pack; also used as expression of excitement in play.
Strike threat - (usually with a foreleg) an aggressive warning prior to an act of physical violence, in a strike threat contact is not made (deliberately); it is used in an attempt to avoid harm to both participants which in the wild could be life threatening.

6 – The Show

A few months passed, the horses were all well settled and Vera had been continuing to train in short sessions during the morning and studying the herd behaviour in the afternoon, as well as her usual, non-horsey lessons. It was winter now so it was too dark to be outside with the horses in the evening and it was so cold she was permanently in her thermal clothes and rain gear. Despite the weather she persevered and was now able to ride Bob in the ménage without a leader and she was sending him round the agility course with ease, their bond was so great that she did not need a bridle and reins to control him, what ever she asked, he did.

After a lovely family Christmas and as she had promised, Mummy started looking for events that Vera could attend with Bob.

'Right' said Mummy as she finished a lengthy session of making phone calls, 'lots of the club shows will only let you do In Hand or Lead Rein classes, because Bob does not have metal shoes on, but there are many others that are happy both for you to compete in ridden classes and to do a demonstration in the arena, the first one is next week'

'OK, what do we do now?' asked Vera

'We will work on your presentation and what you want to say for a couple of days, and work out a routine for the class and the demo, then Thursday you can have a practise run in front of a few friends, if you are happy with that we can get Bob cleaned and Saturday we go' Said Mummy

The week past quickly and it was soon Thursday, Mummy had gathered Babushka and Dedushka (Grandpa in Russian), Grandma, Elsa and Theo as well as Mummy's long time friends, Kiara, Peter and their two children Anna and Joseph. Vera walked in to the ménage with Bob wearing his tack (horse term for saddle and bridle) and proceeded to start her talk.

'…Shaping is the term used to describe a method of training where you break down the final desired outcome into small, easily learnt steps, once the horse has learnt the individual steps you can put them together to get the final behaviour that you had wanted, it takes planning and patience but is very effective for complicated behaviours or ones that don't happen naturally in the horses daily activities…' said Vera.

When she had finished she did a little bow, Peter looked a little puzzled; he was not used to being around horses and held the common belief that horses lived in stables, ate hay and carrots and were a little dumb.

'The problem with normal stabling is that horses are awake about Eighteen hours per day, so if you 'put them to bed' at six in the evening, they have something like Twelve hours in a confined space, that stops them running away if they are frightened, stops them grooming each other, assuming they are stabled separately and they have to poop too close to where they are eating, drinking and sleeping. It greatly increases the chance of them developing a stereotypical behaviour like weaving (also seen in predators in small enclosures at zoos), then instead of trying to find out why the horse is stereotyping, some people might try to stop them doing it by putting up bars, for example… but this usually just leads to the horse getting another bad habit or becoming depressed. If they must be in a stable, target training, can be a bit of a distraction and help prevent boredom' said Vera 'Also, while it is frowned upon to hit a dog or cat with a whip, horses are regularly hit and people excuse it saying that they have thick or tough skin… this is not true, horse skin has more nerve receptors than our own, that's why it moves so much at the slightest tickle, what is more – hitting reinforces fear and due to their size, a frightened horse is a dangerous horse.'

'That is very interesting, I had never thought of that, you should include that in your speech' said Peter

'It is a lot like human learning, isn't it' said Kiara who was a teaching assistant and regularly worked with autistic children (many of whom also find direct eye contact intimidating)

'Yes, all animals can be taught and learn via conditioning and reinforcement, since I started learning about horse training, I have seen many people train all different kinds of animals like, rabbits putting their toys away before dinner and farm animals doing agility or target training' Vera replied.

The next day Vera and her Mummy made the recommended adjustments to her demonstration, gave Bob a good bath and packed up the trailer ready for the morning.

The day of the show, Mummy loaded Bob onto the lorry with William for company and off they went. At the show they were parked amongst the other horses and competitors, all with shiny coats and plaited manes and adorned with leather tack and metal shoes, Vera looked at Bob, her scruffy little gelding with the big scar down one side, he looked so different. Vera stood in the holding ring, waiting for the young handler class, three girls walked past with their ponies, laughing and looking down at Vera.

'You are never going to win anything with that' one girl sniggered pointing at Bob

word of the day:
Perceive - (verb): to become aware of, know, or identify by means of the senses.

'Unless it is fancy dress!' joked another as she patted her pony hard on the neck.

'Do you know research has suggested your pony might perceive you patting her as aggressive and the same as punishment?... We are doing a talk about horse welfare and Positive Reinforcement this afternoon, maybe you should come' said Vera defiantly.

'What?!' exclaimed the first girl

'This is a competition for real horse riders, not someone like you!' declared the other, laughing as they walked off.

Vera started to sob and walked over to the edge of the ring where her mother was waiting to watch the class.

'Mummy, Bob looks so out of place with these horses; he doesn't even look the same species! And I don't look like those other girls either; maybe this was a mistake… I can't do it' cried Vera

'Oh Vera, It does not matter if you look different… why would you want to look the same as everyone else? Just remember why you are here' said Mummy as she cuddled Vera tightly and dried her eyes.

'To show what Positive Reinforcement can do and spread the word about improving horse welfare' Vera stated

'Exactly' said Mummy 'The whole world might not be ready to hear it but the more people you show, the more might think about changing, even if it is just little things like not using spurs or whips or not tying the nose band too tightly; it is all a step to happier horses is it not?... remember most people only look to change if something goes wrong or their current methods are no longer working… even if they do see how well you have done, challenging their beliefs can make them uneasy and look to other people who share their beliefs to get support in discrediting you or justify to themselves why their methods are ok (cognitive dissonance) but you cant force them… They have to consciously decide to reconsider their approach otherwise it wont stick. There will always be a few people that are interested and will go on to research further for themselves and this is our aim.'

'You are right Mummy' said Vera as she walked off to enter the competition ring.

word of the day:
Spurs - (noun): a device that straps to the heel of a boot and has a blunt, pointed, or roweled projection at the back.   **Cognitive Dissonance - (noun) an uncomfortable mental state resulting from conflicting beliefs or beliefs being challenged by another person; resolved by changing beliefs or behaviour, or seeking people with similar beliefs in order to dismiss the challenger (bury your head in the sand).**

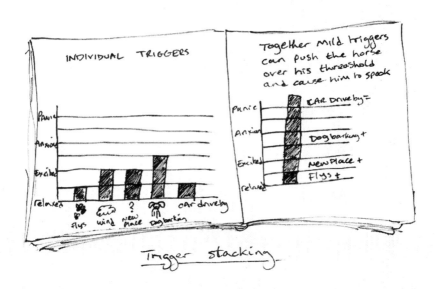

INDIVIDUAL TRIGGERS

Panic

Anxious

Excited

relaxed

flys   wind   new   dog barking   cAr drive by
               place

Together Mild triggers can push the horse over his threshold and cause him to spook

Panic

Anxious   CAR Drive by =

Excited   Dog barking +
           New Place +

relaxed   Flys +

Trigger stacking

Vera did exactly as they had practiced, running up and down in the ring, and much to her delight (and the dismay of the snooty girls she had spoken to) she got Second place.

At One o'clock it was time for the demonstration, Mummy tacked Bob up and Vera rode him into the centre arena. It was a small crowd of about thirty-forty people. Bright lights shone down on the sand and there was a strange scent of popcorn and smoke mixed with horse poop. Taking a deep breath she proceeded to introduce herself and Bob; talking a bit about their journey, on the screen behind them, video footage of Bob's training played silently, Vera could hear people sniggering and whispering, it was those girls again but this time with their parents, a couple of whom got up and left. She dismounted Bob and continued to talk, walking around while Bob stood patiently in the middle.

'I understand that not everyone will be ready to hear or accept what I am saying and that is fine, we all have our own journey to make and it is not for others to judge either way, but I am ready to stand up for what I believe in, and that is better treatment and understanding of my favourite non-human animal, the horse… A year ago I thought horses silly for jumping when, for example, they see a pigeon fly out of a bush in the forest, but now I understand what they call **Trigger Stacking**, what the horse is fine with normally can be scary when added together with other mild annoyances like it being hot, flies biting him or lots of traffic going by… I also understand that they do not generalise well; to prepare Bob for today, we had to practice in different locations around our farm, in front of a crowd of people and with distractions of riding horses and vehicles nearby. Bob has been trained slowly with Positive Reinforcement and I think you will see the amazing results… What I like best is that he has been granted the freedom to choose whether he wants to ride or spend time with me' said Vera with confidence

Whilst Vera had been talking Mummy had removed the saddle and bridle and took it back over to the side, the audience looked perplexed. Vera signalled Bob who came walking over, Vera gave him a rub on the shoulder, before directing him to the seesaw on the agility course, followed by a little jump and walking through a big tunnel with lots of rustling paper, all without batting an eyelid, for her perfect finish, Bob lifted his foreleg, allowing Vera to step up onto his back, then just holding the neck strap for stability, Bob trotted off across the arena and performed a lovely routine including the Spanish Walk, reversing around an 'L' shape and back through the scary tunnel. Vera took a bow and dismounted and then Bob and Vera bowed together, side by side in the spotlight.

> **terms of the day:**
> **Trigger Stacking - used to describe the exposure to multiple stimulus that on their own would cause little or no reaction but together overload the horse's tolerance levels causing what seems like an over-reaction. Generalise - (verb): apply knowledge an experience gained in one situation to another.**

'Thank you' she said

The crowd went wild, clapping and cheering; they all stood on their feet. Lots of people and media representatives waited to speak to Vera and her Mummy, asking how someone so young can be so wise and achieve such things.

'Passion, purpose and being committed to observing and respecting nature and all the species that inhabit it' said Mummy proudly.

Vera demonstrated and competed at three more shows before her eight birthday, also getting her First Prize ribbon. Each show she was advertised to be showing at had a bigger audience and longer question time, the video footage from the shows went viral on the internet and with help from Mummy and Daddy managing her social media pages, Vera became very well know and inundated with messages and requests for tips and advice. At her eighth birthday party and in front of all her family and friends, Vera announced her plans for the next year:

'I want to write a book, and travel the world spreading the message of positive reinforcement. I can use my drawings to explain body language to other children so they can be safe around animals' said Vera

'What about your education?' said Grandpa

'I think it is a brilliant idea, we can incorporate it into your home learning and it can be done from anywhere, there will be plenty of important lessons to be learnt from the other cultures and countries we can visit.' Replied Mummy with a smile and a wink to Vera

'Yes, the world will be my school' exclaimed Vera, throwing her arms in the air and spinning gleefully.

Please remember to always use protective clothing and never enter an animal enclosure without the presence of an adult.

Authors Note

This book is intended as a basic introduction to Learning Theory, and in particular, aimed at horses as whilst many of the other animal training methods have moved on the approach to horses lags behind. The story is intended to encourage improved welfare and treatment of all animals and inspire readers to research further into Learning Theory.

My own horses have each taught me so much because of their highly different personalities, one in particular is so sensitive that to use anything other than positive reinforcement would have tipped her over the edge and made her either shutdown or dangerous to be around.

Rewards are brilliant for all species especially when needing them to do something like see the vet, doctor or dentist. It can also be used for fun and mental activities like tracking scent with their noses, rabbits putting their toys away, horses playing fetch, hamster agility courses, even bees have been trained to do tasks for rewards. The possibilities are endless.

The book contains a lot of moral life messages that are applicable and transferable to other scenarios. It introduces complex equestrian specific terms and psychological language with definitions and illustrations.

There are many groups on social media that can help with this as well as bloggers, vloggers and books.
Follow me on: @positivecultivation for links and more information.

Printed in Great Britain
by Amazon